100 WAYS TO HAPPY

100 WAYS TO HAPPY

SIMPLE ACTIVITIES TO HELP YOU LIVE JOYFULLY

ADAMS MEDIA
New York London Toronto Sydney New Delhi

Adams Media
An Imprint of Simon & Schuster, Inc.
57 Littlefield Street
Avon, Massachusetts 02322

First Adams Media hardcover edition January 2021

ADAMS MEDIA and colophon are trademarks of Simon & Schuster.

For information about special discounts for bulk purchases, please contact Simon & Schuster Special Sales at 1-866-506-1949 or business@simonandschuster.com.

The Simon & Schuster Speakers Bureau can bring authors to your live event. For more information or to book an event contact the Simon & Schuster Speakers Bureau at 1-866-248-3049 or visit our website at www.simonspeakers.com.

Interior design and illustrations by Priscilla Yuen

Manufactured in the United States of America

10 9 8 7 6 5 4 3 2 1

Library of Congress Cataloging-in-Publication Data
Names: Adams Media (Firm) editor.
Title: 100 ways to happy.
Description: Avon, Massachusetts: Adams Media, 2021. | Series: 100 ways.
Identifiers: LCCN 2020034723 | ISBN 9781507215135 (hc) | ISBN 9781507215142 (ebook)
Subjects: LCSH: Happiness. | Self-help techniques.
Classification: LCC BF575.H27 223 2021 | DDC 158.1--dc23
LC record available at https://lccn.loc.gov/2020034723

ISBN 978-1-5072-1513-5
ISBN 978-1-5072-1514-2 (ebook)

Contains material adapted from the following title published by Adams Media, an Imprint of Simon & Schuster, Inc.: *The Book of Happy* by Adams Media, copyright © 2018, ISBN 978-1-5072-1007-9.

CONTENTS

10 | *Introduction*

13 | **WAYS TO HAPPY**
15 | Choose to Think Happy Thoughts
16 | Enjoy a Five-Minute Renewal
18 | Have More Fun
20 | Cultivate Your Uniqueness
22 | Expect the Best
23 | Say No
25 | Listen to Music and Sing Along
26 | Practice Deep Breathing
28 | Sniff a Memory
30 | Release Your Resistance
31 | Attract the People You Want in Your Life
32 | Follow Your Heart
33 | Notice the Wonders of Life
35 | Stretch

36	Relish the Rainbow
38	Feel the Energy of Your Words
40	Drink Water
41	Laugh—A Lot
42	Meditate On Love and Kindness
44	Spread Happiness
47	Attain Natural Bliss
48	Be Grateful
50	Fulfill a Dream
52	Help Your Community
54	Reminisce
55	Expand Your Awareness
56	Write a Check to Yourself
59	Cultivate Opportunities
60	Wear More Color
61	Be Aware
62	Move Past Perfection
64	Transform Doubt Into Courage
65	Trust Your Path
66	Be the Light in the Darkness
68	Stop Complaining
71	Let Go of Negative Body Images
72	Greet the Dawn

74	Follow the 60 Percent Rule
75	Give Your Undivided Attention
76	Don't Dwell
78	Differentiate Feelings and Experiences
79	Speak to Your Soul
80	Write a Haiku
83	Invite Your Inner Child to Play
84	Speak Your Truth
86	Ask for Something
88	Walk Without a Destination

89	Take a Belly Breath
90	Visualize Friendship
92	Walk Away from Drama
93	Eat Your Favorite Food
95	Recognize Your Support System
96	Savor Better Sleep
98	Do the Unexpected
99	Draw Your Inner Critic
100	Accept Responsibility for Your Actions
102	Focus On What's Right in Front of You
103	Sniff Some Lavender

104 | Love Yourself
107 | Dance Around the Kitchen
108 | Nourish Your Skin
110 | Stargaze
112 | Think Globally
113 | Plan Your Dream Vacation
114 | Assert Yourself

115 | Live in the Now
116 | Wish for Happiness
119 | Stop Worrying
120 | Move In, Not On
122 | Toast Yourself
123 | Realize What's Really Important to You
124 | Clarify Your Intention
126 | Choose Love
127 | Visualize Yourself Reaching Your Goal
128 | Bloom Where You're Planted
131 | Use Your Skills
132 | Replace Negative Self-Talk
134 | Honor the Good in Others
135 | Surround Yourself with Meaningful Things

136	Bask in the Sun's Joy
137	Acknowledge Your Feelings
138	Look for the Good in a Bad Situation
141	Share a Funny Joke
142	Meditate for Inner Peace
144	Live Passionately
146	Put a Bamboo Plant in Your Kitchen
147	Snuggle Up
148	Create a Vision Board
150	Take a "Me" Day
151	Acknowledge Your Blessings
153	Live Well
154	Connect to Your Feelings
155	Share the Good
156	Savor Your Memories
158	Shine Bright
160	Smile at Yourself
161	Buy Small Things
162	Write a Blessings List
165	Celebrate Your Strengths
166	Remember That Happiness Is a Journey
168	*Index*

Introduction

Do you find yourself longing for positivity?
Wish you had a little more joy in your life?
Feel like you just need a break from the
negativity that surrounds you?

In today's hectic world, happiness can be tough to find. Fortunately, *100 Ways to Happy* is here to help you find your smile and bring a sense of bliss and balance to your life when you need it the most.

Each of the one hundred exercises throughout the book will help you live the happiest life you can and become more content and worry-free. There are mantras you can recite, meditations you can do, and easy suggestions to help you put your life and activities in perspective, including:

Embrace your uniqueness

Sing along to music

Speak your truth

Get a good night's sleep

These activities, along with a number of inspiring quotations, will help you look for the good things that surround you and find a sense of purpose, belonging, and well-being—no matter what life brings your way.

In a world that can feel not-so-great, *100 Ways to Happy* has just what you need to find joy. So take a deep breath and get ready to embrace happiness.

WAYS to HAPPY

Attitude is a choice.

Happiness is a choice.

Optimism is a choice.

Kindness is a choice.

Giving is a choice.

Respect is a choice.

Whatever choice you make makes you.

Choose wisely.

ROY T. BENNETT,
American author

Choose to Think
HAPPY THOUGHTS

Even if you aren't normally a happy person, thinking happy thoughts is a skill that can be learned.

Work on choosing to think positive thoughts and seeing the proverbial glass as half full rather than half empty.

So the next time someone says something rude or does something that makes you upset, respond with kindness and respect. Keep that positive vibe going through your intentions and actions in whatever you do. The more often you choose to be happy, the happier you'll actually feel.

Enjoy
A
Five-Minute
Renewal

You try to eat well, exercise, and get enough sleep—at least a few hours every night—but sometimes the daily grind doesn't leave much time for self-care. Before you become overwhelmed, set aside some time each day to rest, relax, and recharge and focus on what makes you happy. Throughout the day, use this breathing exercise to reconnect with your own source of happiness:

1. Sit with a straight spine, palms facing upward on your thighs.

2. Inhale, softly making the sound of *So*.

3. Exhale, making the sound of *Hum*. Do this So Hum breathing for one minute. (This mantra, from the Sanskrit, translates as "I am that.")

4. Rest your consciousness in the silence for four minutes as your thoughts gravitate toward contact with the Divine.

5. Feel your life-force energy being recharged and reinvigorated and reconnect with your happy place.

HAVE MORE FUN

Fun is light,
enjoyable, and energizing. It broadens your
horizons and limits your focus so you're not worrying
about anything too serious. If you don't have enough fun
in your life, look at your calendar for the next week and
find a time to do at least one thing just for recreation—
play tennis with a friend, go salsa dancing, visit a used
bookstore. Having it scheduled will help you relax a
little during the rest of the week, knowing
that you're doing something to
tend to your happiness.

Also,
encourage yourself
to weave smaller bits of fun into
your everyday experience—eat dinner on
the patio, drive home the pretty way, play with
the kids on the playground instead of checking your
phone. These moments will lift your spirits and make
everything else you do feel a little more effortless.

Cultivate

YOUR

UNIQUENESS

Your values, beliefs, feelings, and opinions—what you bring out into the world of your inner being rather than what the world brings you—partly define you. Foster happiness by letting go of a professional or personal self-image that depends on labels that others may have put on you.

Become more aware of your inner magnificence by doing the following:

> *Be courageous and confident.*
>
> *Express your uniqueness through creative ideas.*
>
> *Listen to the voice of your soul (intuition).*
>
> *Speak your truth.*
>
> *Love your journey more than any destination along the way.*

As you do these things, focus on your own unique inner attributes, talents, traits, wisdom, and gifts. Then figure out how you might use them for your own happiness and that of others.

EXPECT
the BEST

*Since energy cannot be destroyed,
neither can your dreams.*

If you desire a life of abundance—whether it be in health, happiness, or finances—it is yours. If you ever feel low, like good things aren't coming your way, remind yourself that you deserve everything you desire. Keep striving for your happiness and eventually it will come. Know that you are already worthy and enough.

Say No

It's easy to say yes—people like you when you say yes to the things they want or need. It's tougher to say no, but sometimes saying no is just the thing you need to feel happier.

If you have a hard time saying no, stand in front of a mirror and practice saying, "No, I just can't," and then turning and walking away. You never again have to give in when you know you don't want to do something or when you know something is not a good idea. Practice until saying no is as easy as saying yes, and enjoy the happiness that saying this little word can bring.

The art of being happy lies in the
power of extracting happiness
from common things.

HENRY WARD BEECHER,
American abolitionist and pastor

Listen to Music
AND SING ALONG

Have you ever noticed how good you feel when you hear certain songs or how an old tune can bring back a flood of happy memories?

That's because music is a mood enhancer. Listening to music releases serotonin (our favorite feel-good hormone) into your system and makes you feel happy. In addition, singing a song triggers a tiny organ in your inner ear called the saccule. It's connected to a part of your brain that registers pleasure, making you feel good no matter how good of a singer you are!

Practice Deep Breathing

From the moment you awaken your mind begins chattering with a steady stream of thoughts. Establish a positive mental state by counting a cycle of deep and slow breaths for five minutes or more. Make the count of your exhalation twice as long as the inhalation.

Mindful breath work is a surefire way to calm the noise in your mind, slow the mental babble, and center your thoughts. Deep breathing can be done anytime during the day when you have a free minute or two. Before an early-morning ritual of breath work, note the following:

> *Avoid eating for several hours*
> *(easy when you do your practice upon awakening).*
> *Drink only water one half hour before practice.*
> *Wear loose clothes.*
> *Align your head and spine for correct posture.*

Eating and drinking can cause stomach upset, and you don't want your clothes to bind you as you practice deep breathing. Deep breathing detoxifies your body and oxygenates your cells while easing away stress and tension. It strengthens the lungs, heart, and immune system, and also elevates mood, boosts stamina, and generates mental acuity.

SNIFF A MEMORY

The connection between scent and memory begins before you're even born and develops as you grow. Your nose learns to detect thousands of scents and to associate certain odors with special memories.

Two olfactory receptors in your nasal passages carry odors to the limbic system (the ancient, primitive part of the brain believed to be the seat of emotion). Odors that bring up pleasant memories lift your mood and foster happiness, which contributes to good health, enhances creativity, and boosts problem-solving abilities.

Keep a vial of essential oil that you associate with a pleasant personal memory or choose lemon (for cheerfulness), lavender (for stress-relieving clarity), or rosemary (for energy). On a facecloth folded in half and then half again, place a drop or two on the top fold.

1 Close your eyes.

2 Hold the scented cloth under your nose.

3 Allow a fond memory to rise in your thoughts.

4 Inhale gently to the count of four.

5 Hold to the count of four.

6 Exhale to the count of eight and repeat at least three times.

Use this ritual anytime you feel the need to return to a happier emotional state.

RELEASE YOUR
Resistance

Have you heard the phrase,
"What you resist persists"?

In other words, if you resist feeling free and happy by holding on to negative emotions, your body will learn how to remain in a state of resistance. This is fine if you are truly being threatened, but you are not meant to be in a state of resistance for very long.

Free yourself of this resistance by announcing, "All resistance melt freely from me now." As you recite this mantra, see resistance melting, kind of like an ice cream cone on a hot day or a Popsicle in the sun.

ATTRACT *the* PEOPLE YOU WANT *in* YOUR LIFE

If you are seeking loyalty and trust in your friendships or in a romantic relationship, first cultivate those qualities within yourself and then demonstrate them to others—in doing so, you become a magnet for exactly what you want. Similarly, if you seek a gentle, loving person as a life partner, avoid someone with a mercurial, volatile, or temperamental nature. Although opposites do sometimes attract, you'll most likely be happiest with a kindred spirit.

Follow Your Heart

Many people have been told to do one thing,
but their hearts steered them to another.
If something feels right in your heart,
it probably is right for you.

In your mind you may doubt your choices or abilities, but your heart usually gently tugs you back to what feels right. When you're conflicted about a decision, tell yourself, "My heart leads me right now; I listen to what feels right."

Go with this. Listen. Trust that your heart knows the way to happiness. Your heart is highly intelligent. The more you listen, the stronger your ability to do what feels right will come through.

Notice the Wonders of Life

Incredible things are happening all around you all the time!

Just for a moment, notice the wonders of life: Look at the way light shimmers on dewdrops clinging to an elaborate spider's web, smell the scent of lilacs after a hard rain, watch the majestic flight of eagles, savor the taste of a freshly cut watermelon, gaze at the pattern of a piece of gum stuck to the pavement, admire the vibrant color of a peacock feather, hear the sizzle of a marshmallow toasted over a crackling fire, etc. Noticing life's little details will fire up your imagination and your natural inquisitiveness about the world.

Everyone wants to live on top of the mountain, but all the happiness and growth occurs while you're climbing it.

ANDY ROONEY,
American radio and TV writer

Stretch

You know how stiff your body feels when you finally get out of a chair after hours of crunching numbers or going through email? Fortunately, it only takes a few minutes to stretch. Some stretches can even be done while sitting in a chair or standing in front of your desk. If you happen to have a yoga mat, take it with you on your break or your lunch hour to a private, peaceful area and do some stretches. You'll feel rejuvenated, flexible, centered, and happier.

Relish the
RAINBOW

Whether you call the newest healthy food craze a Buddha bowl, hippie bowl, rainbow bowl, or bowl of ancient grains and veggies, it's guaranteed to deliver plenty of balanced nutrition to keep your body and brain healthy and happy.

For a lunchtime ritual, create a vitamin- and mineral-packed nourishing bowl of rainbow-colored foods. Include fresh or cooked veggies, fruit, protein, and fat but limit the carbohydrates. Follow these simple steps:

1. Establish a base of colorful, freshly washed leafy greens such as kale, spinach, and a variety of lettuces in a midsized bowl.

2. Add raw veggies such as green broccoli, yellow sweet corn, or sliced purplish beets, or cooked vegetables such as green lentils and others of various colors and sizes.

3. Drop in protein-rich ingredients (grilled meat, hard-boiled eggs, or tofu).

4. Add a source of healthy fat (fish, avocado, nuts).

5. Sprinkle nuts, seeds, or berries over the top, and toss together if you desire to mix the ingredients.

Feel the ENERGY of YOUR WORDS

A big part of living a fearless and happy life is learning how to communicate effectively. Mantras teach you how to become more energy-focused in your communication, rather than word-focused.

Sure, words have energy, but just because you hear words that have low vibrations (e.g., "This sucks!") doesn't mean you have to react to them. Notice the energy without judgment.

Rather than focusing on the meaning of the word, observe the energy and say **"I am learning to communicate in peaceful and empowering ways."**

For example, if someone says **"This sucks,"** observing the energy gives you information (guidance) that this person may feel overwhelmed or stuck in a situation.

Then you can respond with **"Sounds like you feel stuck."** This response is a much more effective way to free them than if you attempt to fix their issue or take on their frustration yourself.

39

DRINK WATER

Staying hydrated gives you more energy, improves your skin's texture and color, and gives your body what it needs to function properly.

Even mild dehydration can have cognitive effects on your mood, decrease your memory, and impact brain function. In fact, many people mistake symptoms of dehydration for symptoms of depression!

If you are feeling lethargic, have difficulty concentrating, or have trouble remembering things, you may need to drink more water. When you get enough water, your body will feel healthier and happier.

Laugh—A Lot

Laughing is the cure for what ails you.

Laughing has amazing benefits, including beating back a tide of stress hormones (cortisol, in particular), giving your body a healthy break, lowering your blood pressure, strengthening your immune system, and generating the release of endorphins (those wonderful happiness hormones). Laughter also provides a physical and emotional release, making you feel cleansed afterward. And it's a great internal workout for your body!

41

Meditate on Love and Kindness

Science suggests that compassion may have a profound, evolutionary purpose because we humans have mirror neurons that react to other people's emotions and trigger in us a desire to help.

Radiating compassion without discrimination makes you stronger, more resilient, and instills greater happiness.

The following meditation guides you from celebrating loving-kindness toward yourself, to celebrating four other people, then to all beings.

1. Use a breathing technique to induce a calm, centered state of mind.

2. Offer a prayer, such as, "I dedicate the virtues of myself for the benefit of all."

3. Think of four people to whom you will send love and then formulate an affirmation to help you arouse loving-kindness in your heart: "I am wanted and loved. I forgive myself and others. I feel my heart full of love. I hold in my heart the peace of the Divine. My loves call forth love, peace, and joy in all hearts."

4. Feel the loving-kindness toward yourself.

5. Visualize each of the four people. Think of them swaddled in love, peace, and happiness as you radiate those feelings to them.

6. Think of the four directions the wind blows and then radiate love in all directions to beings of all spheres and realms.

SPREAD
HAPPINESS

Happiness in your life doesn't have to be purely internal. You can find great joy through making other people happy.

Simple acts of kindness, such as holding the door for someone, letting someone go ahead of you in line, or paying for another person's cup of coffee are ways to spread happiness. Happiness is contagious. You can literally change the climate of a room through acts of kindness.

After you help someone, repeat the following phrase:

"Appreciation and gratitude pulsate through me now."

As you recite this mantra, notice how the energy of the words rests on your heart. Breathe deeply as you send loving thoughts to yourself and the world around you.

There is no
path to happiness:
happiness is the path.

GAUTAMA BUDDHA,
Indian spiritual leader and founder of Buddhism

Attain Natural Bliss

Nature blooms all around you and can grant you immense happiness if you allow it to.

When you're out in nature, say to yourself the mantra, "I receive fully the joy and nourishment nature brings"—this will help your brain produce some "happy chemicals" like serotonin and dopamine. Mantras not only support the production of these chemicals; they also shift your brain waves into more calming states.

This mantra is great for those times of day when you are transitioning from indoors to outdoors (e.g., checking your mail or walking to your car). It encourages you to fully soak in the ample benefits nature provides.

BE GRATEFUL

When you focus on what you love about your life, your positive emotional brain fires up. This creates a focused, positive feeling free of worry and fear, a state of mind that allows you to truly enjoy moments of happiness.

Before you go to sleep each night, write down at least five things you're grateful for and pause to re-experience the pleasure each one brings you. Focus on what is making you feel lucky and good about your life, and you'll soon find that you feel more positive in general and that you begin to slow down and savor the good times.

Fulfill
A
Dream

When you put your dreams on hold to help someone else attain his or hers, your selfless action is praiseworthy. However, if you wait too long to chase your own visions, conditions for achieving them may change, your priorities might shift, or you may abandon all hope of ever attaining your dreams. Alternatively, perhaps you still secretly nurture the idea of achieving your cherished dream and just thinking about it fills you with excitement, energy, and a sense of adventure. A ritual might help jump-start it again. Begin this process by writing your dream on a card in felt-tip marker. Holding the card in your palms, do the following:

1. Mentally banish fear; release limiting and discouraging beliefs.
2. Kindle feelings of self-worth for your desire to have that dream.
3. Ask the universe for what you want; use precise language.
4. Open yourself to opportunities that make achieving your dream possible.
5. Let go and trust that your dream has moved from a state of improbable to certain attainment.

Help
YOUR
Community

Your soul wants to contribute to something greater than you.

As a human being, you can have all the money and fame in the world; however, if you do not feel like you are contributing to the world in some way, you will feel unsatisfied. Taking time to contribute to your surroundings can change all of this.

Whether it's taking a moment to pick up a piece of trash, donating a few items, or volunteering at a local charity, contributing to your community not only helps other people but also makes you happier.

After you complete a day of giving back, reaffirm the happiness you experienced in helping others by saying, "I am a contributor to my community."

Reminisce

The happiness that can come from reminiscing about happy memories is as real as the feelings that happened during the actual event.

In fact, people who frequently reminisce about positive life events are the most likely to be happy. So take photos, make scrapbooks, bring home souvenirs, call an old friend, watch your favorite movies...do whatever you need to do to relive those positive memories.

EXPAND YOUR AWARENESS

It can be so easy to get caught up in other people's descriptions of happiness.

A *Facebook* post, bit of celebrity news, or Snapchat photo compels you to live someone else's moment (even if it's fixed or filtered or edited), and it can give you a false impression of what true happiness is. When you focus too much on other people as a measure of your own happiness, you inevitably disconnect from your source of happiness—yourself.

Happiness is an internal state of being, not an external place you have to find. Recite, "As I expand my awareness, energy flows freely through me." This will redirect and expand your awareness to your internal source of happiness.

Write a Check to Yourself

DATE: 11/11/2011

PAID TO THE ORDER OF: _Crusaller love_ $

_____ DOLLARS

Paid in full   _Law of Abundance_

56

Writing an abundance check to yourself might take only a minute or two of your time, but it could pay off substantially in a newfound prosperity.

Follow these steps to perform a new moon check ritual once a month.

1 On a blank check (a real one or one you create to look real), write today's date.

2 Make it out to your full legal name.

3 Leave blank the dollar amount box and line, but on the signature line, write: "Law of Abundance."

4 Write in the memo sector: "Paid in full."

5 Take out the check at the beginning of each new moon and hold the paper in your palms while you visualize the dollar amount you desire to attract that month.

6 Feel happiness when you are inspired with ideas for opportunities for making money as well as when money flows in. Don't forget to express gratitude (write thank-you notes and tuck them into a box where you keep the check).

Happiness cannot be
traveled to, owned, earned,
worn, or consumed.

Happiness is the spiritual experience
of living every minute with
love, grace, and gratitude.

DENIS WAITLEY,
American motivational speaker and author

Cultivate
Opportunities

If you are concerned that your opportunities are limited—
perhaps you have a belief that there are only so many jobs,
or that all the good jobs are taken—then tell yourself,
"Opportunities come my way easily."

Be mindful that if you tie up your time and energy with something you don't like, or a job that may be draining you, that choice could interfere with your happiness and your opportunity to create something new. Recite this mantra daily and avoid making choices that don't lead to your true bliss because you fear you will never have another chance. Opportunities are always available. Allow this mantra to increase your ability to trust this.

Wear More Color

Studies have shown that color can enhance your mood and make you feel better about yourself.

The takeaway? While black may be slimming for your body, it isn't doing much for your mind. Get out of your black clothing rut and add a little color to your wardrobe! You'll notice an improved sense of confidence, and happiness will follow.

Be Aware

A simple shift in perception can move you closer to happiness. All you have to do is become aware of yourself in this moment.

Awareness means consciousness. To be aware is to notice and be awake to your surroundings. If you are distracted or consumed by thinking, your awareness may be low. Choose to increase it by taking a moment to pause and listen to your breath. Listen and feel your breath moving in and out of your body. Your breath will anchor you to the present moment. Being aware and fully present makes it easier to recognize happiness when and where it's available.

Move PAST PERFECTION

If you love to get things right every time and invest in high standards and lofty goals, falling short isn't an option. But when it happens, the voice of your inner critic might sound off loud and clear.

Letting go of the need for perfection might seem almost impossible until you figure out how to tamp down the inner critic and move past the need to control. Once you can move past that compulsion, you open space in your being to feel joy.

Light a candle scented with sweet orange, a scent favored in Europe, the Middle East, and China during the tenth century to foster relaxation and warm, comforting, and peaceful feelings. Deep breathe for six breaths and then relax and focus your thoughts on things that you can do successfully rather than perfectly, which is so much easier. Repeat this process until you feel peace settle in your bones.

TRANSFORM DOUBT
Into COURAGE

Think of doubt as streaks on a window.
They can create an unpleasant distraction from
what you're trying to see outside.

Doubts have the same effect on your energy—they distract it and make it congested. When you begin to doubt yourself, tell yourself, "Now that courage, strength, and love are in motion, all shadows of doubt are erased."

Similar to wiping a window clean, use this mantra to transform doubt into courage and happiness. It's best to sit or stand up tall when you're reciting it. Allow yourself to really feel the mantra in your body.

Trust Your Path

There is no right or wrong path.
All paths lead to the heart.

Live in love and happiness and your path will be illuminated for you. Like most paths, don't be surprised if there are twists and turns filled with unhappiness. Stay focused on the moment and repeat this mantra:

"Uncertainty awakens me now. I trust this path."

State the mantra when you start to second-guess your decisions or question your capabilities. It's not that you won't change your mind from time to time, but maintain trust that the path unfolding for you has its source in the eternal flow of life.

BE THE

Light

IN THE

DARKNESS

When faced with darkness, become a beacon of light.

Be an exemplar of humility, civility, patience, compassion, kindness, sincerity, and—above all—calmness. Acting with positive energy doesn't just make other people happy. It makes you happy too! You might even make a few friends along the way.

1. Sit with a straight spine. Close your eyes and tune in to your heart as you breathe naturally in a slow pattern.

2. Visualize a beautiful temple. See yourself crossing a peaceful lake that washes away all negativity as you prepare to enter the temple.

3. Let the temple light embrace you as the inner sound of tinkling bells rings out your presence.

4. Call forth an individual with whom you've had a negative encounter.

5. Welcome him or her into the temple's sacred space.

6. Observe how the darkness dissipates once you act with compassion.

7. Fix your thoughts on the good in all hearts.

8. Rest in the healing light of friendship.

STOP
COMPLAINING

Seeing as the brain has a tendency to focus on the negative, complaining may in fact be a natural human reaction. Still, that doesn't mean complaining is the best reaction.

Dwelling on the worst of the world is not good for your body or your mood. Besides, when has complaining ever gotten you anywhere? All it does is reinforce negativity. So rather than complaining about something, try to focus on something else, something positive. You'll be happier.

I think happiness is what
makes you pretty. Period.
Happy people are beautiful.
They become like a mirror and
they reflect that happiness.

DREW BARRYMORE,
American actress

Let Go of Negative Body Images

There is no one "correct" body type.

Sure, you should strive to be as healthy as you can, but if you feel comfortable in your own skin and you're happy with your life, other people's opinions of body types shouldn't matter. Don't let other people tell you you're not beautiful or that you could be more beautiful if you only did this or that. Your opinion of your body is the only one that matters. If you are not happy in your own skin, then take steps to improve yourself, but only if you truly desire to make those changes.

Greet the Dawn

Since ancient times, yogis have hailed the hour and a half before sunrise as the most auspicious time of the day. Some believe that accessing the positivity and power of deeper meditative states is easier in the predawn when your mind is still.

Before throwing off those covers to drink water, attend to hygiene, exercise, and eat breakfast, take some time to linger in that quiet space between sleeping and wakefulness with a morning ritual that focuses on gathering positive energy. This space holds for you gifts of extraordinary phenomena, including:

Intense imagery

Audible sounds of nature, voices, and music

Taste sensations

Touch sensitivity

Otherworldly scents of incense or florals or unidentifiable smells

A heightened sense of presence

Follow the
60 PERCENT RULE

Perfection isn't possible. But many people pursue perfectionism with such vigor that it can actually be damaging.

It's time to adjust that thinking. According to the 60 percent rule, if your friendships, work life, and relationships are 60 percent "perfect," then you are doing something right. Keep up the good work! Pushing for perfectionism will cause you unneeded stress and anxiety—instead, embrace the imperfect and feel happier.

GIVE YOUR UNDIVIDED ATTENTION

Some days it seems that everybody is clamoring for your attention. But when it comes to family members, it's important that you give it to them.

Ten minutes often is not enough to really get started talking, but it shows your loved ones that you care deeply about what troubles them and that you want to help. Even if your help is just listening to them vent, do it. You can always set aside another ten minutes to continue the discussion at a later time. Consider the alternative. Brushing them aside for more urgent matters sends the wrong signal. Make time for loved ones before they leave your nest. Isn't it true that you are happiest when you know that they are happy too?

DON'T DWELL

The past is a valuable thing; it holds valuable memories and teaches us lessons.

Learn from those lessons and learn from those mistakes…and then let them go. If something bad has happened, see it as an opportunity to learn something you didn't know. If someone else made a mistake, see it as an opportunity to be forgiving and understanding. The past does not define you. Think of the past as practice and training, letting you learn lessons so that you don't repeat them. Don't dwell on the bad aspects of the past and don't live in the pain of old hurts. Move forward!

Differentiate Feelings and Experiences

Happiness is a feeling that makes you feel lighthearted and allows you to experience pleasure.

Like other emotions, happiness can have a range. On one end, you can be elevated, perhaps giddy, while on the other end, you may feel quietly content. One is not better than the other—both are experiences of happiness. Joy tends to be less dependent on situations or circumstances. Joy is a state of being. Sure, you might have moments where you feel sad or even angry, but those emotions do not destroy your overall joy for living. Both are vitally important to your overall well-being. Remind yourself of this by saying, "Happiness is a feeling; joy is an experience. I choose both."

Speak to Your Soul

So many people try to be a happy human. Fair enough. But try to focus on being a happy soul instead by repeating, "I am a happy soul."

Happy souls have no problem asking for guidance and support. Unhappy souls feel alone, unsupported, and disconnected. The next time you feel unsure about what to do, rather than ask your brain, ask your soul: "Soul, what would you have me do?" Your soul speaks to you through a hunch or a feeling, sometimes even visually or auditorily. Embrace each as a message guiding you toward a happy life.

Write a Haiku

A haiku is a three-line poem that many people use as a meditation aid. They can also just be a lot of fun to compose and bring joy to both the writer and reader.

The first line is always five syllables, the second line is seven, and the last line is five again. Follow these tips to create a meditative haiku:

- To write a haiku in English, concentrate on simply capturing a fleeting moment, evoking a beautiful image of the ephemeral quality of life.

- A haiku often focuses on a moment in nature, and typically includes a word that lets the reader know what season it is. For example, the word *daffodils* would indicate spring.

- It's traditional in Japanese haiku to use a *kireji*, or a "cutting word." This word is used to show juxtaposition between two ideas in the haiku, or to signal the end of one of the images. In English, this is typically done with a punctuation mark, like a dash or period.

- Use your haiku as a focus during your meditation exercises. Let it bring you peace and happiness.

Now and then it's good to
pause in our pursuit of
happiness and
just be happy.

GUILLAUME APOLLINAIRE,
French poet

Invite Your Inner
CHILD TO PLAY

*Somewhere deep inside you is the inner child
you forgot about long ago.*

Find that wild child again and do what used to make you happy. Was it painting, kicking a soccer ball around, or dancing in front of the sliding glass door where you could see your image? Perhaps you were the kind of child who loved playing with Play-Doh, calculating hopscotch squares, jumping rope, playing a musical instrument, or drawing for hours under a tree.

Afraid someone might see you? Forget about that. Find an old Hula-Hoop. Put it around your waist and start swerving in circles. Stretch out your arms. Whirl and twirl. Close your eyes. Enjoy the movement. Feel young. Feel renewed. It's exhilarating.

SPEAK
your
TRUTH

If someone from the past has caused you to doubt the validity of your worth in the world and silenced your voice, find ways to re-emerge, gain confidence, and speak out.

In the greater universe, we may be tiny specks, but in this world, you are just as important as every other person. To empower your authentic voice, join a book club, community forum, or social group where disseminating ideas and expressing personal opinions are encouraged. Or reflect on your voice by doing the following ritual:

1. Wash a blue lapis lazuli stone (a symbol of wisdom and truth) in a mild saltwater solution and let it dry in the sun to absorb solar energy.

2. Lie in Corpse Pose (a yoga position in which you're flat on your back, palms up at your side) and place the stone over the center of your throat.

3. Meditate on your inner divine nature and the happiness that arises when you use your voice.

Ask for Something

Whether it's asking a family member to pass a napkin, a friend for a favor, or your husband to take the kids so you can go to yoga, challenge yourself to open your mouth and make a request today.

This is related to, but different from, asking yourself what you most need in this moment—it's taking the insight you gain from a moment of reflection and saying it out loud. Making such a request takes awareness. It also takes allowing yourself to be seen as having needs. Which means it can also take courage (especially if you are an "I can handle it" type). But speaking up will bring you comfort, empowerment, and happiness.

WALK WITHOUT *a* DESTINATION

Here's a way to get some movement while also building your relationship with your intuition— a relationship that is vital to your happiness.

At some point each week, take yourself on a walk with no particular destination in mind. Every time you come to a crossroads, take a look in each direction and head the way that's calling to you the most. You're not trying to get anywhere— you're simply letting your gut lead the way. This exercise is a tangible way to reprogram the well-worn paths of your thoughts and can open you up to delightful surprises—a coffee shop you've never noticed before, for example, or a chance encounter with a dog or a neighbor who's not on your usual route.

Take a
Belly Breath

*When you're feeling stressed and unhappy,
take a moment to repeat the simplest of
mantras:* Ahhhhh.

This simple sound is far more powerful than you may think. You're giving yourself permission to release that pain in your neck (or anywhere else!) and return to being happy. Muscle tension is often a reflection of energy that is being held hostage in the body. As a result, the body becomes depleted of oxygen. Circulating fresh oxygen deep into your body helps you release this pent-up energy. Go ahead, fill up your belly with breath. Inflate it now, fully (like a balloon). Allow your mouth to open slightly and release a nice *Ahhhhh* sound.

VISUALIZE
Friendship

*Friends are essential to true happiness.
No one can walk through life alone
and expect to be happy.*

Examine your life for the friends who helped you in some way to blossom. Express why you appreciate someone who has touched your life in profound and positive ways in an act of gratitude. Send out joy and appreciation and they will return to bless you.

1   Find a comfortable position in a chair or on a mat. Sit erect with eyes closed.

2   Take several deep, cleansing breaths.

3   Mentally invite in the friends who are walking with you on this journey of life—people who've touched you in a special way.

4   Focus on each person, explaining his or her particular gift to you and why you view it as a blessing.

5   Elaborate on how the blessing affects your life today.

6   Visualize the next friend and repeat the process. Do this until you've addressed each in turn.

7   Thank your friends; vow to write a note of appreciation to each during the week (and follow through on that promise).

8   Rest in the warm happy feelings of being valued by your special coterie of friends. As you go forth into your day, do good for others as your friends have done for you.

WALK AWAY
from Drama

Interpersonal drama is created from conflict, insecurity, and pain.

Perhaps you live in a family where gossip and conflict are common. Or maybe your workplace environment is like this. These types of family and/or work dynamics can get quite heated with tension. In an attempt to cope with the situation, you may be forced to detach yourself from it all. This may work to some degree but tuning out or walking away is only a part of the process. As you walk away, remind yourself that you are "Neutralizing drama now" by uttering that phrase to yourself. See yourself as becoming neutral to what is happening. This means the drama does not impact you either way. In other words, you are able to observe without being drawn in.

EAT YOUR FAVORITE FOOD

You know how happy you feel when you're eating your favorite food—that's why it's your favorite.

Cook or order that one dish that just puts a smile on your face. It could be comfort food from your childhood, an exotic creation you first tasted on vacation, or even a savory palate-pleaser you learned to cook on your own. Happily savor every bite of that Moroccan chicken tagine, New England crab cake, Midwestern meatloaf, Southern fried chicken, or whatever is your favorite.

If you want happiness for an hour,
take a nap.
If you want happiness for a day,
go fishing.
If you want happiness for a year,
inherit a fortune.
If you want happiness for a lifetime,
help someone else.

CHINESE PROVERB

Recognize Your
SUPPORT SYSTEM

Always going it alone can be incredibly stressful and can lead to a lot of unhappiness in your life.

Taking on worries and concerns without regard for yourself makes life seem heavy and challenging, rather than light and interesting.

If you believe you are unsupported, change your thinking by saying, "The universe generously supports me." The universe will reflect this message back to you. Realizing that you have the support of more than just the things and people around you can alleviate much of your stress and unhappiness.

SAVOR BETTER SLEEP

Clearing away the chaos of the day isn't always easy.

Sometimes just getting to sleep proves difficult. But sleep is how the body and brain heal and cells renew. Yoga nidra ("yogic sleep") involves deep conscious relaxation to release muscle tension and emotions trapped in your subconscious after a hectic day.

Do yoga nidra as your body hits those cool cotton sheets. Deep, restorative sleep will soon engulf you.

1. Lie on your back in bed.

2. Focus your attention on the right foot and ankle.

3. Move your attention slowly up the whole limb. Relax it.

4. Repeat the process for the left lower limb.

5. Mentally check in with your pelvis, tummy, and torso.

6. Shift your attention to your right shoulder and guide your attention along the arm down to your hand and fingers. Feel the whole limb relax.

7. Repeat step 6 for the left shoulder, arm, and hand.

8. Breathe in, breathe out with an awareness of all the sensations in your body.

9. Turn onto your right side, where left-nostril breathing cools your body (lying on your right side means the left nostril is higher than the right and air flows easily and without restriction through the left). Relax.

10. Roll back onto your back. Deepen the relaxation until you cross the threshold into restorative sleep.

DO THE UNEXPECTED

If you want to feel alive and happy, get a little crazy.

Do something spontaneous such as having a picnic (even in the front yard) or doing a totally out-of-the-ordinary activity like dancing under the light of the full moon or lying on fresh powder and making a snow angel. Maybe you take a day off and visit an architectural salvage yard, spend an afternoon antiquing, or take the subway to the end of the line just because you can.

Whatever is out of the ordinary for you, give it a shot. You'll find youthful exuberance taking over and replacing the humdrum routine that might be bogging down your days. Make it a weekly ritual to find this happiness again and do something spontaneous.

Draw Your Inner Critic

Everyone's got at least one mean voice inside their head.

You know, the one who says things like "What were you thinking? Maybe there's just something wrong with you. You really screwed that one up."

Whenever you're feeling unhappy and deeply negative, pull back the curtain on your inner critic by drawing a picture of her or him. How old is she? Does he wear glasses? What kinds of clothes do you imagine her in?

If you can personify the voice, you can see that it's not you. Which means you'll give her a little less stock the next time she starts in on you.

Accept Responsibility FOR Your Actions

You can't be happy if you're denying guilt or some other hidden emotion. You must be fully honest, both with yourself and others, to be happy.

If you find yourself struggling to open up and tell the truth about a difficult subject, tell yourself, "I am willing and ready to take full responsibilities for my actions."

As you consider your actions, keep in mind your intention is not to admit fault but rather to restore trust and respect with another or yourself. Offering an apology is so much more than simply admitting your mistakes. A true apology gives you a way to free yourself from carrying the burden of guilt and disappointment. Sincere apologies have no alternative agenda and are incredibly powerful energy tools for rebuilding trust and harmony.

Focus On What's Right in Front of You

*Name three things that are going on
right in this moment.*

Perhaps you're sitting some place comfortable, the sun is shining, and your pet is curled up nearby. This is an exercise you can do anytime you notice your stress levels rising, because allowing yourself to see what's right in front of you, right now, helps keep you grounded in this moment. And what a relief that is!

Sniff Some Lavender

If you're having a bad day, sniff some lavender to restore your serenity.

It's easy to see why lavender is one of the most popular scents in aromatherapy. (Scents like citrus, rose, and sandalwood are also pleasant. When you smell them, they can trigger particular memories or experiences because your olfactory nerve carries their scent straight to your brain.) There are many ways to enjoy lavender: Use freshly crushed flowers set out in a bowl, set some reeds in a diffuser pot with a splash of lavender essential oil, light some lavender-scented candles, simmer lavender potpourri, or put out sachets of dried lavender. Allow the scent to lift your mood and bask in a sense of happiness.

Love Yourself

You cannot be happy if you are not happy with who you are.

Bring happiness to yourself
by repeating the mantra,

"I love being me."

Being you means you are able to allow your own thoughts, feelings, and beliefs to emerge with honor and respect. This does not mean you have to act on every little thing. Notice if you start to compare yourself to others or question your abilities and strengths. Take these doubts as a sign that you may be veering from your sense of being. Your path is always being shaped by the way you respond to what is happening inside of you. To get back on your course, put your attention on the now and recite this mantra.

True happiness is to enjoy the present, without anxious dependence upon the future, not to amuse ourselves with either hopes or fears but to rest satisfied with what we have, which is sufficient, for he that is so wants nothing. The greatest blessings of mankind are within us and within our reach. A wise man is content with his lot, whatever it may be, without wishing for what he has not.

SENECA,
Roman philosopher

Dance Around the Kitchen

Start your day with a little salsa, mambo, cha-cha, or your favorite dance steps as you make your way over to measure the coffee, add the water, and turn on the pot.

Dance until the coffee is ready. Have a cup and then dance some more! Start your fancy footwork in your kitchen and jig throughout your house. If you have to leave for work, dance your way to your dressing room and keep moving while you get ready. Dance over to pick up your purse, briefcase, and car keys...and then dance right into the garage. Keep moving and feel your smile emerge.

Nourish Your SKIN

*You feel happier and more empowered
when you look and feel great.*

Your outer appearance reflects the inner you. The condition of your skin is closely related to your overall well-being. Follow these basic steps to keep yourself at your best, inside and out:

- Meditate to feel peace and happiness.
- Deep breathe to bring more oxygen to your cells.
- Get enough sleep.
- Eat nutritious foods.
- Drink lots of water.
- Limit your skin's exposure to the sun, environmental pollution, and toxic substances.
- Find and use a nourishing all-natural face cream or make your own with rich emollients such as almond oil, vitamin E oil, coconut oil, beeswax, and shea butter. A few drops of essential oil for fragrance are optional.
- If you want luminous beauty that glows throughout your lifetime, look inside yourself. Frequent contact with your inner luminosity will manifest externally, in joy, serenity, and grace.
- Bust stress by eliminating stressors where possible; sink deeply into moments of tranquility.

Stargaze

Looking up at a sky full of stars is not only a meditative exercise that helps you feel more calm and centered; it also teaches you perspective.

Contemplating the vastness and distance of space and the universe gives you a new angle on your life and problems... and stargazing helps you discover the beauty of nature too.

Stargazing can also be a kind of meditation; the calm peacefulness of gazing up at the stars helps quiet your mind and the stresses of your day. As an additional bonus, the time spent outside—even as little as twenty minutes—will be a big happiness booster.

THINK GLOBALLY

Happiness in your life doesn't have to be limited to only you, your loved ones, or your community.

Remember, you are part of a large global community as well and their happiness can affect yours. Remember your global community with the mantra, "May all beings everywhere be happy and free, and may the thoughts, words, and actions of my own life contribute in some way to that happiness and to that freedom for all."

This mantra reminds us that no one is really free from suffering entirely until we are all free. It gives you a tangible tool to help you move through the overwhelming experiences that our busy world often sends our way. Remember, fear cannot survive in love. They cannot both exist.

PLAN YOUR DREAM VACATION

The anticipation of an event can often bring just as much happiness as the actual event, so start planning the vacation of your dreams now!

Even if you don't currently have the funds to take the trip, start looking into the details. You'll notice your spirits start to lift.

Maybe you've always wanted to go trekking in the Himalayas or visit a rainforest. No matter your ideal destination, start researching the various aspects of your trip and formulate a plan on how to make your dream a reality.

ASSERT YOURSELF

Having a strong voice not only protects you but builds confidence in yourself.

Foster this strong voice by choosing to speak up and assert yourself. Don't be afraid to speak up, ask for help, or let people know if something is bothering you. Break any silence and let go of secrets that you've been hiding.

Suppressing your thoughts and feelings can lead to high levels of stress, resentment, and dissatisfaction with the way things are unfolding in your life, preventing you from being truly happy. It can also live in your body like trauma, holding unpleasant memories in place. So strengthen your voice and build your courage. You'll be happier for it.

Live in the Now

Worrying about the future is an energy drainer.

It's a counterproductive means for attempting to control an outcome. The more you attempt to control, the more stuck, emotionally fragile, and overwhelmed you may feel. Treat your body as an ally. What is it trying to tell you?

Deferring to your body as a channel of light and love brings you to the present moment, where fear and worry do not exist. Help open this channel wide by repeating the mantra,

"I feel the flow of light now."

If you tend to focus on what you have to do or what is left undone, consider reciting this mantra at the beginning and end of each day.

WISH for HAPPINESS

Wishing happiness for all beings can take practice.

There's a special kind of meditation that is used for cultivating this ability. It's called metta meditation.

There are variations, but in general this is how you practice metta:

1. Sit in a comfortable, seated position for meditation.

2. Close your eyes, and follow your breath as it goes in and out several times.

3. Say this to yourself: "May I be happy. May I be healthy. May I know peace."

4. Bring to mind someone you love dearly. Hold this person in your mind's eye. Say this wish: "May you be happy. May you be healthy. May you know peace."

5. Bring to mind someone who is an acquaintance whom you have good feelings toward and don't know very well. Perhaps it's someone who works in the same building as you, or the person at the post office who always helps you mail your packages. Hold this person in your mind's eye and say: "May you be happy. May you be healthy. May you know peace."

6. Now repeat this for all beings: "May all beings be happy. May all beings be healthy. May all beings know peace." When you are finished, open your eyes.

Happiness is when what you think, what you say, and what you do are in harmony.

MAHATMA GANDHI,
Indian activist

Stop Worrying

We're a society of worriers, but in reality most of the terrible things that we envision happening never do.

We're afraid of what might happen (or not happen) with respect to things we can't change (or won't be able to change) and what other people think about us. We worry and we hesitate, and as a consequence, we wind up thinking longer about doing something rather than just doing it. Meanwhile, weeks, months, and years pass, and we are still worried and still unhappy.

If you want to be happier, put aside fear and worry and do something! Start something; take a first step. The only thing you should worry about is wasting your days and your life and not doing what you dream about doing.

MOVE IN, NOT ON

When it comes to forgiveness,
there is no moving on;
there is only moving in.

Your attitude and life experiences may change, but it is only when you move deeper into yourself that you will truly be liberated. The next time you hear yourself saying "I need to move on" or "If only I could just stop thinking about this person or situation," consider reciting "I choose to let go by moving in rather than moving on."

Allow this mantra to draw your awareness inward. As you move inward, your perception will shift, and you may realize that there was never anything to let go of in the first place. The thing you thought you needed to let go of turns into something you have learned to appreciate and respect.

Toast Yourself

Even if you don't have a special occasion like an anniversary or birthday to celebrate, break out a good bottle of champagne or prosecco (nonalcoholic works just as well) and a fancy champagne flute.

To make it even more special, put a strawberry in the drink. You can do this by yourself or with a loved one. Give a toast to honor something you are proud of or happy about today. A little sense of occasion on an otherwise boring night will make you feel special. Don't forget that just waking up in the morning is a reason to celebrate.

REALIZE WHAT'S REALLY IMPORTANT TO YOU

Millions of people live their lives without a sense of direction.

Unless you know what's really important to you and what you want out of life, how are you going to know where you are going, how to get what you want, and what your life purpose is?

Think of ten things that are most important to you (for example, family unity). Then make each item as specific as possible. Instead of family unity, maybe you really mean eating meals together or doing the chores together. Refine the ten things on your list until you know exactly what is most important to you. These are the things that will make you happiest. Knowing what they are can help you make better choices in your personal life journey.

CLARIFY YOUR INTENTION

You've always wanted to go to Peru, see the Andes, the Amazon rainforest, and Machu Picchu. You can't explain the attraction, yet when someone asks you where you'd most like to go on vacation, that country pops right up on your lips.

Write out your intention in a clear statement of purpose, and then you are ready to break your purpose into smaller, incremental goals. Write down your goals, including a reward for reaching each one. Follow this plan with the following affirmation: "I intend to visit Machu Picchu in May next year." Stay focused. Do not doubt and you'll get there, because every intention must be answered. Here's a twice-daily ritual to strengthen your specific intention, whatever it may be.

1. Light a joss stick of dried perfume paste or incense to sanctify the space.

2. Sit in your favorite meditation posture with eyes closed and declare your specific intention.

3. Feel worthy. Trust that you've been heard.

4. Visualize your desire manifesting and feel the emotional high.

5. Seize opportunity when it comes; give thanks.

CHOOSE LOVE

Overfocusing on your problems or worrying about the future disables your ability to tune in to love and happiness.

If you question your relationships or expect that certain things in your life are unlikely to work out, then you'll strip away at the love inside of you. Rather than continue these patterns, choose to focus on self-love and learn to listen to the needs of your body and spirit.

Self-love is not as complicated or overwhelming as you might think. The act of pausing and taking a drink of water is a demonstration of love. Noticing the temperature of the water as it runs over your hands while washing dishes is a way to connect to love. Love is in the moment; it is right now, as you are reading this. It is recognizing the happiness all around you and celebrating that happiness. Pay attention to how your body responds to the experiences and interactions of your day without judgment. Soak up moments that offer you connections to the moment. These are all part of love.

Visualize Yourself Reaching Your Goal

What's your primary personal goal? Is it to practice self-care, socialize more, or earn more money?

Whatever it is, write out an affirmation for achieving it. For example: "From now on at mealtimes, I will eat one-third less" or "I will walk for a half hour each day." Try to keep your affirmation succinct and to the point. That way, it will be easy to recall and repeat at least three times during the day. The more specific your affirmation, the more effective it will be in helping you attain your goal.

Bloom where you're planted

You bloom wherever you are planted.

For example, you may have an idea or expectation in your mind that before you can bloom you have to be in a certain phase of your life, have a particular situation, or have more money. This is a belief, not a truth. Allow your happiness to bloom wherever and whenever you can by reminding yourself always that "I am blooming."

You can blossom in any area of your life. Whether you are a mother with small children, someone exploring a new hobby that brings you joy, or are in the middle of your career blooming, you are thriving and growing through your relationship with energy. By simply choosing to breathe into this moment, you are blooming.

*Success is getting
what you want;
happiness is wanting
what you get.*

DALE CARNEGIE,
American author

Use Your Skills

Fear of being judged can hold you back from putting your skills and assets out there for the world to see.

Be proud of the skills, knowledge, and experience you have, and put them to good use going after the things that will make you happy.

Don't hesitate to toot your own horn! If you have been working behind the scenes, supporting the success of others, perhaps it is time to make a shift and allow yourself to manifest some of the creative talents and insights you have gathered. Begin the process now!

Replace Negative Self-Talk

The greatest obstacle to achieving what we want and finding happiness is ourselves.

Time and again we talk ourselves out of being happy, sending negative vibrations throughout the universe. This is an exercise to do if you find that something seems to be blocking your ability to attract what you want.

1. Sit quietly and clear your mind, concentrating on your breathing.

2. When your mind is calm and unburdened, review your thoughts during the past twenty-four hours.

3. How many of these thoughts were positive and affirming?

4. How many of these thoughts were negative self-talk or not accurate portrayals of reality?

5. If the negative thoughts have been outweighing the positive ones, flip the equation. Strengthen your positive thoughts, making them as specific as possible.

Honor the
GOOD IN OTHERS

The word namaste, *which you'll often hear at the end of meditation or yoga class, is actually a mantra that means "The light in me sees the light in you."*

Another translation would be "The good in me sees the honorable and good in you." When you recite this mantra, know that it does not apply exclusively to people. You can state it to a tree, animal, or even an idea. It's a gentle way to bless the world and spread happiness throughout the universe.

SURROUND YOURSELF with MEANINGFUL THINGS

Whether your sanctuary is your home or your office, determine what makes you happy and then choose furniture, art, wall colors, books, and pictures of people who inspire you. Perhaps it's a settee you found in a vintage shop that lifts your spirits. Or your grandmother's drop-leaf claw-foot table that she always loved.

Items with meaning should find a place in the interiors where you live and work precisely because they hold special memories and significance for you. Like everything in the universe, those well-loved pieces are permeated with subtle joyful energy from the people who've loved you and also used and loved those pieces. Fill your space with them and embrace the sense of happiness that they will bring to your sanctuary.

Bask in the Sun's Joy

The sun is one of the greatest sources of happiness and joy on earth.

Not only does the sun give you vitamin D, which is essential to maintaining a positive mood and healthy bones, it also strengthens your energy field. Think about how good you feel after sitting (even briefly) in the sun.

Give thanks to the sun for your happiness and try to take time to go outside for a few minutes a day (particularly if it's sunny). Make this self-care ritual a part of your daily routine.

Acknowledge Your Feelings

There is pain in life.

At some point in your glorious life, you will be unhappy, hurt, or depressed. These things are natural and part of everyone's human experience. The most important thing during these times is to not beat yourself up about feeling the way you do. Feeling sorry or embarrassed about feeling bad will not help you; in fact, those additional negative feelings may just drag you down even further.

Instead, acknowledge your feelings—they are nothing to be ashamed of. Accepting the pain and difficulty of a situation is one of the ways to help yourself get out of it and back on the path to happiness.

LOOK FOR THE GOOD IN A BAD SITUATION

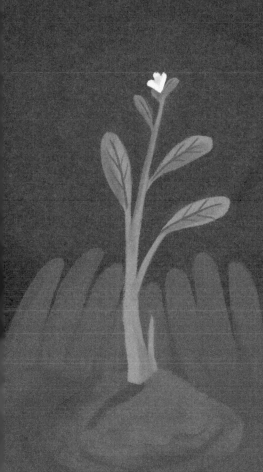

Every one of us has experienced losses—some more extreme than others—but there is often a seed of triumph hidden in those losses.

It may be hard to see at first, but it's there. Try asking yourself: "What is the good in this? What lesson can I take away? How can I share my knowledge with others?" Bring to mind two or three events that may have seemed totally awful up to this point and write down only the good things and/or the benefits gained from each. Looking for the brighter side is a great habit to develop— you'll become a happier and more compassionate person.

Happiness consists more in small conveniences or pleasures that occur every day, than in great pieces of good fortune that happen but seldom.

BENJAMIN FRANKLIN,
American founding father

Share a Funny Joke

Heard any good jokes lately?
Have you tried passing them on?

Telling a funny joke is a terrific way to cheer up others, defuse tense situations, add much-needed levity in times of stress, and generate some positive effects on your health. Memorizing a joke and telling it to others is just one way to cultivate a sense of humor. Did you know that laughing may actually reduce your risk for heart disease and can mitigate damage incurred when you are experiencing deep distress and pain? Also, some sources say that while sniffles, sneezes, and coughing are contagious, laughter is even more so. So if you want to feel good, cultivate the ability to laugh at stressful situations and share that laughter with a friend.

MEDITATE for INNER PEACE

In Buddhism, inner peace isn't a static condition; it's a dynamic state brimming with insight, perception, knowledge, and compassion.

The following instructions are the foundation for the meditation and contemplation practiced by saints and sages over time throughout the world. They can bring you a joyful peace.

1. With eyes closed, direct your attention to the space between your brows. This will be your focal point for this meditation. Gently gaze into that space without straining.

2. As thoughts or emotions arise to threaten your peace, don't try to reason, deny, or argue them away. That would be conflicting and counterproductive, derailing your meditation. Don't be hard on yourself but rather practice patience and loving-kindness.

3. Maintain a detached awareness of what arises during meditation.

4. Hold on to the awareness of that inner peace. Carry that joyful serenity unhindered into your day.

Live PASSIONATELY

Anyone can meander through life, going with the flow and not feeling much of anything. However, those people are almost always unhappy. Be passionate and proclaim to the world, "Passion, I am that!"

Passion gives you the ability to see the world in color. When you are focused on comparing and contrasting, you are in black-and-white (all-or-nothing) thinking. Black-and-white thinking narrows your focus. As this occurs, you may become tied to time and responsibilities. When you view things from passion (color), you are living in the flow (timelessness). Sure, you still get things done, but your life is fueled by your passion rather than your attachment to controlling the course of your day.

PUT *a* BAMBOO PLANT *in* YOUR KITCHEN

Put a lucky bamboo plant on your kitchen counter where it will happily enjoy some warmth.

Even if you don't have a green thumb, you can successfully grow this plant. It doesn't need much light and will thrive in water (as long as the water is clean and kept at the same level). According to the ancient Chinese tradition of feng shui, the lucky bamboo (not actually a bamboo at all but a member of the *Dracaena* genus) creates harmony wherever it is placed. Its numerous long green leaves grow out of a single stalk. If you work from home, put a six-stalk plant in your office to attract prosperity or a three-stalk plant in the bedroom to ensure longevity, wealth, and happiness.

Snuggle Up

If you are like many people,
as a child you had a little pillow or a security
blanket that got you through the night.

As an adult facing a crisis, you may wish you had something tangible like that to give you comfort.

If you don't have a favorite blanket or pillow, look in the linen closet and see if there's a comfy throw, a worn afghan, or a silky coverlet you could use. Then, the next time life is not going your way, seek comfort in what's familiar and what makes you feel safe and happy—wrap yourself in your blanket and let your inner child feel comforted.

Create a Vision Board

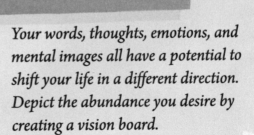

Your words, thoughts, emotions, and mental images all have a potential to shift your life in a different direction. Depict the abundance you desire by creating a vision board.

1 Take a large piece of poster board and draw three rows of three boxes each (nine equal boxes). Label the boxes in the top row with *money*, *fame*, and *love*. Label the boxes in the second row with *knowledge*, *career*, and *helpful people*. Label the last row with *health*, *balance*, and *creativity*.

2 Cut and paste images that reflect for you abundance relative to each box. The idea is to create a vision for the life you want with a belief that what you can see, you can manifest.

3 Put your vision board next to your desk and feel happy and excited and worthy each time you look at it. Trust that what you see you are going to get.

Take a "Me" Day

There are many things we celebrate in life: babies, milestones, birthdays, etc. Every once in a while, though, it's important to take the time to say, "I'm celebrating me today."

This mantra reminds you to acknowledge your growth, even the little things. You work hard and deserve to reward yourself with your very own special occasion day. So shut off your phone and spend some time assessing and appreciating where you're at. Today, celebrate your strengths and your willingness to forgive yourself and others. See the honor and courage required in these actions.

ACKNOWLEDGE YOUR BLESSINGS

To say that you are blessed is far more than saying you have good luck or fortune.

Acknowledge your blessings simply by repeating "I am blessed" to yourself. To be blessed is to be aware that you are holy and therefore have received grace. It is important to keep this in mind as you recite this mantra. Mindfulness allows you to be grateful for who you are right now, rather than who you hope to be, and can bring a calm happiness into your life. Another version of this mantra is "We are blessed." This statement gives you the ability to see and honor the grace in others as well.

Let us be grateful to the
people who make us happy;
they are the charming
gardeners who make
our souls blossom.

MARCEL PROUST,
French author

Live Well

To be well, you have to live well.

Tell yourself you are doing just that by saying the mantra,

"I live well,"

and allow it to bring happiness into your life. Rather than focusing on what you *can't* do, this mantra reminds you that you are both the author and the illustrator of your life. Before repeating the mantra, ask yourself: What does living well look like for me? How does it feel? What would I imagine myself doing if I were living well? Repeat this mantra several times and allow yourself to visualize what this would look, feel, and sound like.

CONNECT to YOUR FEELINGS

So many of us have been taught that our emotions are a sign of weakness or a cue that something might be wrong.

This could not be further from the truth. Your emotions are the way you are able to connect with yourself and other human beings. Being in touch with them and acknowledging their power can only bring you happiness.

These connections represent true strength and are the ultimate form of protection. No one can harm you when you are honest, sincere, and allow yourself to move through (i.e., shed or release) all of your emotions (even the negative ones).

Share the Good

Have you ever had a positive or kind thought and held yourself back from sharing it?

Perhaps you loved a yoga class but never took the time to express it to the teacher, or you were touched by the kind gesture of another but felt awkward letting them know.

Remind yourself to spread joy by telling yourself, "I have something good to say and I choose to say it!" Giving other people compliments or thanking them for their time and attention brings happiness to both parties. Let's face it, even the most confident people could use a pat on the back now and then. Make a point to let others know they are doing a good job and watch how your happiness increases too!

SAVOR
YOUR
MEMORIES

Your brain is wired to scan for and remember adverse events—this "negativity bias" helped humans adapt to threats in their environment. But what was great for our evolution can now be a root of stress and anxiety. To help re-train your brain, dedicate some time to reveling in good memories.

1 Sit quietly and call up a happy moment.

2 Relive that memory in the greatest detail you can muster, and let the good feelings soak into your cells.

3 Appreciate the positive things you experience even more, which boosts gratitude and contentment.

SHINE BRIGHT

*Happy people tend to shine on
rather than move on.*

To move on means to push your feelings down or hold them back, and then go about your way. To shine on means to pause and allow yourself to fully experience what is coming up without judging it. While you pause, quietly repeat "Shine on!" to yourself in order to stay in the right mindset.

You might feel a twisted feeling in your stomach, tightness in your chest, or clenching of your teeth. Shining on means to trust the inner guidance of your body. Digest your emotions and you will grow (shine) from the experience. Ignore or guard yourself from your emotions and you may find yourself recycling (stuck in) the same emotions and experiences.

SMILE
at Yourself

It may sound silly, but smiling causes an emotional response in your body that can actually make you feel happier.

Smiling at other people can make them and you feel happier, but smiling at yourself in the mirror can have the added effect of boosting your self-esteem and self-love. Imagine smiling at yourself in the mirror every morning—think about what that would do for your confidence and mood throughout the day!

BUY SMALL THINGS

Instead of buying the latest smartphone, the coolest new car, or the best new laptop, buy several small things: fancy chocolates, a few nice candles, some music for your phone, etc. It will actually make you happier to indulge in frequent small pleasures than to buy more extravagant (and expensive) delights. After all, you don't get twice as much happiness from buying a car that is twice as expensive as another model! Use some of that money to pay for a weekend away. You'll get far more satisfaction from your getaway weekend than you would from the luxury car.

Write a Blessings List

162

Laughter, love, health, friends, family, money, spiritual growth, and a loving and powerful support network represent a cornucopia of blessings that suggest a prosperous and joyful life. In the fast-paced environments that characterize the modern world, you might not realize how blessed you are.

Inside a red envelope, write a list of your blessings. Insert a dollar. Close the envelope and rub it between your palms to generate positive energy that will attract more of the same. Place the envelope in the northeast corner of your sacred space. Intensify the energy by placing a crystal on top of the envelope and cover both with a red cloth. Each week during the year, open the envelope, review your blessings, and add more to your list. Shake the dollar and the red cloth, and as you reassemble the envelope, recite: "I attract an abundance of all good things that bless me and mine."

If you look to others for fulfillment,

you will never be fulfilled.

If your happiness depends on money,

you will never be happy with yourself.

Be content with what you have;

rejoice in the way things are.

When you realize there is nothing lacking,

the whole world belongs to you.

LAO TZU,
Chinese philosopher and founder of Taoism

Celebrate
YOUR STRENGTHS

Research has shown that focusing on your strengths decreases depression and increases healthy behaviors. Identify your strengths by asking yourself two questions:

1. In what areas do I feel strong?
2. In what areas am I getting stronger?

These areas can be as simple as feeling strong in a particular skill such as cooking, drawing, or reading. You may have strong interpersonal skills, or maybe you are pretty good at getting organized or using a computer. Take a moment now to acknowledge and celebrate what you are good at, as well as the skills you look forward to developing.

REMEMBER THAT HAPPINESS IS A JOURNEY

If you look back over the past week and remember moments of happiness (even if they're only fleeting) but find that your memories are dominated by moments of stress, anxiety, frustration, exasperation, sadness, resentment, jealousy, impatience, worry, concern, or anger, grab a cup of your favorite tea, put your feet up, and consider this: Happy isn't something you feel only after you've accomplished everything you want to achieve in life. It's available to you during every step of the journey... but you make the choice of whether or not you experience that happiness.

Index

Abundance
    attracting, 148–49, 163
    law of, 57
    life of, 22, 163
    mantra for, 163
    writing check for, 56–57
Actions, responsibility for, 100–101
Actions, unexpected, 98
Affirmations. *See also* Mantras
    for goals, 127
    for intentions, 125
    for loving-kindness, 43
    for meditations, 43
    specific affirmations, 127
Apollinaire, Guillaume, 82
Apologies, 101
Aromatherapy, 103
Attention, undivided, 75
Attitude, 14, 121
Attraction, of desires, 57, 124–25, 133, 146, 162–63
Attraction, of kindred spirits, 31
Awareness
    expanding, 55, 61
    love and, 126
    mantras for, 55, 121
    of present moments, 126

Balance, finding, 10–11, 149
Bamboo plants, 146
Barrymore, Drew, 70
Beauty
    body image and, 71
    happiness and, 70
    inner beauty, 70, 109
    of nature, 110–11
    nourishing, 109
Beecher, Henry Ward, 24
Bennett, Roy T., 14
Blessings
    acknowledging, 151, 162–63
    of friendships, 91
    list of, 162–63
    mantras for, 151, 163
    reviewing, 163
    of world, 134
Bliss, 10–11, 47. *See also* Happiness; Joy
Body image, 71
Breaks
    lunch breaks, 35
    from phone, 19, 150, 161
    vacation getaways, 113, 124–25, 161
Breathing exercises
    belly breaths, 89
    benefits of, 17, 26–27, 89, 97, 109

deep breathing, 26–27
for happiness, 17
mindful breathing, 26–27
for sleep, 97
Buddha, Gautama, 46
Buddhism, 46, 143

Calmness, 27, 43, 47, 67, 111.
    See also Peace
Career
    60 percent rule for, 74
    drama and, 92
    growth of, 129
    vision board for, 149
Carnegie, Dale, 130
Celebrations
    of happiness, 126
    of loving-kindness, 43
    mantra for, 150
    of milestones, 150
    of self, 43, 122, 126, 150, 165
    of strengths, 150, 165
Centering techniques, 27, 35, 43, 111
Chaos, removing, 96–97
Check, writing to self, 56–58
Choices, wise, 14, 15, 32, 59, 78, 123, 126
Colors, wearing, 60
Comfort, finding, 63, 87, 102, 147
Comfort food, 93
Communication tips, 38–39
Community, global, 112
Community, helping, 52–53, 112
Comparisons, avoiding, 55, 105, 145
Compassion, 42–43, 67, 139, 143
Complaints, stopping, 68–69

Conflict, eliminating, 92, 143
Contentment, 11, 78, 106, 157, 164.
    See also Happiness
Contributions, 52–53, 112
Control, avoiding, 63, 115
Courage, 64, 86–87, 114
Creativity
    celebrating, 165
    enhancing, 29
    expressing, 21
    fun and, 18–19, 83
    opportunities for, 59
    success and, 131
    talents and, 131
    uniqueness and, 21
    vision board for, 148–49
    writing haiku, 80–81

Dancing, 83, 98, 107
Darkness, illuminating, 66–67
Dawn, greeting, 72–73
Deep breathing, 26–27. *See also*
    Breathing exercises
Depression, easing, 40, 137, 165
Desires
    asking for, 51, 79, 86–87, 124–25
    attracting, 57, 124–25, 133, 146, 162–63
    focus on, 22, 123
    visualizing, 124–25
Destination
    goals and, 34
    journey and, 21, 34, 88
    vacations and, 113, 124–25, 161
Divine, contact with, 17, 43, 85
Doubt, erasing, 32, 64, 85, 125

Drama, reducing, 92
Dreams, fulfilling, 50–51

Emotions
    acknowledging, 137
    connecting to, 154
    differentiating, 78
    negative emotions, 30
Empowerment, 39, 85, 87, 101, 108
Endorphins, 41
Energy
    boosting, 27, 29, 40, 64, 136
    essential oils for, 29
    hydration for, 40
    positive energy, 67, 73
    recharging, 17, 35
    thriving with, 129
    of words, 38–39
Enough, being, 22
Enough, having, 106, 164
Essential oils, 29, 103
Exercise, 17, 35, 73, 88. See also Yoga
Expectations, 22, 126, 129

Family
    conflicts in, 92
    focus on, 75
    requests to, 86
    support from, 95
    unity of, 123
Fatigue, reducing, 40
Fear, releasing, 49, 51, 112, 115, 119
Feelings, 78, 137, 154. See also Emotions
Feng shui, 146
Foods, favorite, 93
Foods, nutritious, 36–37, 109

Forgiveness, 43, 77, 121, 150
Franklin, Benjamin, 140
Friends. See also Relationships
    60 percent rule for, 74
    appreciating, 90–91
    attracting, 31
    blessing, 91
    focus on, 74, 75
    loyal friends, 31
    requests to, 86
    support from, 95
    trusting, 31
    visualizing, 90–91
Fulfillment, 50–51, 164
Fun, 18–19, 83
Future, worries about, 106, 115, 126

Gandhi, Mahatma, 118
Global community, 112
Global thinking, 112
Goals
    affirmations for, 127
    clarifying, 124–25
    destination and, 34
    journey and, 34
    reaching, 127
    setting, 123–27
    specific goals, 123, 125, 127
    visualizing, 127
Good, seeing, 134, 138–39
Good, sharing, 155
Grace, 58, 109, 151
Gratitude, expressing, 45, 48–49, 57–58, 152
Grounding techniques, 27, 102
Guidance, seeking, 39, 43, 79, 159
Guilt, releasing, 101

Haiku, writing, 80–81
Happiness
    art of, 24
    choosing, 14, 15, 78
    contentment and, 11, 78, 106, 157, 164
    experiencing, 58, 78, 167
    finding, 10–11, 22, 42–47, 63, 78, 82,
        104–5, 132–33
    fostering, 15, 21, 29
    as journey, 166–67
    mantras for, 47, 55, 105, 117
    money and, 53, 129, 161, 163, 164
    obstacles to, 132–33
    path to, 32, 46, 61, 65, 105, 137
    spreading, 44–46, 91, 116–17, 134, 155
    state of, 55, 118, 130, 166–67
    success and, 130, 131, 167
    wishing for, 116–17
"Happy chemicals," 47
Harmony, creating, 101, 118, 146
Health, improving, 22, 27, 29, 96–97, 117
Healthy food, 36–37
Heart, following, 32, 65
Helping others, 45, 52–53, 94. See also
    Kindness
Hobbies, 83, 129
Honesty, 101, 154
Honoring others, 134, 151
Hormones, 25, 41, 47
Hydration, 40

Immune system, 27, 41
Inner beauty, 70, 109. See also Beauty
Inner being, 21, 85, 109, 159
Inner child, 83, 147
Inner critic, 63, 99

Inner peace, 142–43. See also Peace
Intentions
    affirmations for, 125
    clarifying, 124–25
    setting, 15, 123–27
    specific intentions, 123, 125, 127
Intuition, 21, 88

Jokes, sharing, 141
Journey
    destination and, 21, 34, 88
    goals and, 34
    happiness as, 166–67
    life journey, 91, 123, 166–67
Joy. See also Happiness
    choosing, 78
    finding, 10–11, 42–47, 63, 78
    hobbies and, 83, 129
    manifesting, 109
    from nature, 47
    spreading, 91, 155
    from sun, 136

Kindness
    acts of, 45, 52–53, 67
    helping others, 45, 52–53, 94
    loving-kindness, 42–43, 143
    mantra for, 45
    meditating on, 42–43, 143
    showing, 14–15, 42–43, 45

Lao Tzu, 164
Laughter, 41, 141
Lessons, learning from, 77, 138–39
Life
    of abundance, 22, 163

Life—*continued*
    blossoming in, 128–29, 152
    details of, 33
    flow of, 65
    life journey, 91, 123, 166–67
    living well, 153
    mantras for, 153
    observing, 33
    passionate living, 144–45
    visualizing, 153
    wasting, 119
    wonders of, 33–34
Light
    channel of, 115
    in darkness, 66–67
    flow of, 115
    seeing, 134
    shining, 66–67, 158–59
    visualizing, 67
Love
    awareness and, 126
    channel of, 115
    choosing, 126
    expressing, 42–43, 58, 104–5, 126
    fear and, 49, 112, 115
    meditating on, 42–43, 143
    self-love, 104–5, 126
Loving-kindness meditation, 42–43, 143

Mantras. *See also* Affirmations
    for abundance, 163
    for appreciating nature, 47
    for awareness, 55, 121
    for blessings, 151, 163
    for bliss, 47

    for celebrations, 150
    for communication, 38–39
    for courage, 64
    for global thinking, 112
    for happiness, 47, 55, 105, 117
    for kindness, 45
    for living in moment, 115
    for living well, 153
    for moving inward, 121
    for nature, 47
    for opportunities, 59
    for renewal, 17
    for resistance, 30
    for seeing good, 134
    for stress, 89
    for support, 95
    for tension, 89
    for trusting path, 65
Meaningful items, 135
"Me" day, 150
Meditations
    affirmations for, 43
    benefits of, 109
    for intentions, 125
    loving-kindness meditation,
        42–43, 143
    metta meditation, 116–17
    for peace, 142–43
    stargazing, 110–11
Memories
    enhancing, 29, 40, 103
    essential oils for, 29, 103
    reminiscing about, 54
    savoring, 29, 54, 156–57
    scents and, 28–29, 103

special memories, 135
Mental acuity, 26–27
Metta meditation, 116–17
Mind chatter, slowing, 26–27, 99
Mindfulness, 26–27, 59, 151
Moments, focus on, 82, 102, 106, 115, 126
Money
    attracting, 148–49, 163
    gratitude for, 57
    happiness and, 53, 129, 161, 163, 164
    for small things, 161
Mood, enhancing, 25–29, 40, 60, 103,
    136, 160
Moving inward, 120–21
Moving on, 120–21, 158–59
Music, 11, 25, 107

Namaste, 134
Nature
    beauty of, 110–11
    benefits of, 33, 47, 110–11
    details in, 33
    joy from, 47
    mantra for, 47
    nourishment from, 47
    observing, 33
    walks in, 88
    wonders of, 33
Negativity
    body image, 71
    complaints and, 68–69
    letting go of, 10–11, 71, 99, 167
    negative emotions, 30
    negative self-talk, 132–33
    resistance and, 30

reviewing, 132–33
Nutrition, 36–37

Opportunities
    cultivating, 51, 59
    ideas for, 57, 59
    learning from past, 77
    mantra for, 59
    opening self to, 51, 59
    seizing, 125
    trusting, 59, 149
Optimism, choosing, 14
Outdoors, appreciating, 33, 47, 110–11.
    See also Nature

Pain, releasing, 76–77, 89, 92, 137, 141
Past, releasing, 76–77
Patience, 67, 143
Peace, finding, 42–43, 63, 109, 142–43
Perceptions, changing, 61, 121, 143
Perfectionism, releasing, 62–63, 74
Perspectives, new, 11, 111
Phone, break from, 19, 150, 161
Play, time for, 18–19, 83
Pleasure, experiencing, 25, 49, 78, 140, 161
Poetry, writing, 80–81
Positive energy, 67, 73
Positive thoughts
    choosing, 15
    focus on, 49, 54, 69, 99
    reviewing, 132–33
    strengthening, 10–11, 133
Prayer, 43
Present, being, 33, 58, 102, 106, 115, 126
Priorities, setting, 51, 123

Problems, solving, 29, 111, 126
Prosperity, 57, 146, 163
Proust, Marcel, 152

Rainbow foods, 36–37
Relationships. *See also* Friends
    60 percent rule for, 74
    attracting, 31
    focus on, 74, 75
    loyalty in, 31
    questioning, 126
    romantic relationships, 31
    support system, 95
    trust in, 31
Relaxation, 17, 19, 63, 96–97
Reminiscing, 54. *See also* Memories
Renewal, 16–17, 83, 96–97
Requests, making, 51, 79, 86–87, 124–25
Resistance, releasing, 30
Respect, showing, 14, 15, 101, 105, 121
Responsibility, accepting, 100–101
Rituals
    for achieving dreams, 51
    daily rituals, 27, 72–73, 125, 136
    self-care rituals, 17, 27, 29, 85, 108–9,
        127, 136, 150
    for setting intentions, 125
    spontaneity for, 98
    writing check to self, 56–57
Romance, 31. *See also* Relationships
Rooney, Andy, 34
Routines, 98, 108–9, 125, 136. *See also* Rituals

Sacred spaces, 67, 163
Sanctuary, 135

Saying no, 23
Scents, 28–29, 103
Self
    celebrating, 43, 122, 126, 150, 165
    centering, 27, 35, 43, 111
    forgiving, 43, 121, 150
    grounding, 27, 102
    rejuvenating, 17, 35
    smiling at, 160
    toasting, 122
    writing check to, 56–58
Self-assertion, 114
Self-awareness, 55, 61
Self-care, 17, 27, 29, 85, 108–9, 127, 136, 150
Self-confidence, 60, 85, 114, 160
Self-esteem, 160
Self-image, 21
Self-love, 104–5, 126
Self-talk, 132–33
Self-trust, 32, 65, 159
Self-worth, 22, 51, 85
Seneca, 106
Serenity, 103, 109, 143
Shining on, 158–59
Sincerity, 67, 101, 154
Singing, 25. *See also* Music
Skills, using, 21, 131
Skin, nourishing, 108–9
Sleep, improving, 11, 96–97, 109
Slowing down, 49, 96–97
Small things, buying, 161
Smiling, 160
Snuggling, 147
Soul, blossoming, 152
Soul, speaking to, 21, 79

Spiritual experiences, 58, 95, 163
Spontaneity, 98
Stargazing, 110–11
Strengths, celebrating, 150, 165
Stress
    breathing exercises for, 26–27, 89, 97, 109
    mantra for, 89
    reducing, 41, 109, 114, 141
    relieving, 27, 29, 89, 95–97, 102
    scents for, 29
    support system and, 95
Stretches, 35, 83
Success, 130, 131, 167
Sunshine, 109, 136
Support system, 95

Talents, 21, 131
Taoism, 164
Tension, 27, 29, 89, 95–97, 102. *See also*
    Stress
Thoughts
    global thinking, 112
    happy thoughts, 15
    mind chatter, 26–27, 99
    negative thoughts, 10–11, 71, 99, 132–33,
        167
    positive thoughts, 10–11, 15, 49, 54, 69,
        99, 132–33
    reprogramming, 88
    reviewing, 132–33
    slowing, 26–27
Time, wasting, 119
Toasts, making, 122
Trust
    mantra for, 65

    in opportunities, 59, 149
    in path, 65
    in relationships, 31
    restoring, 101
    self-trust, 32, 65, 159
Truth, speaking, 11, 21, 84–85

Unexpected actions, 98
Uniqueness, 11, 20–21

Vacations, planning, 113, 124–25, 161
Vision board, creating, 148–49
Visualizations
    of desires, 124–25
    of friendships, 90–91
    of goals, 127
    of light, 67
    for living well, 153
    vision board for, 148–49
Volunteerism, 53

Waitley, Denis, 58
Walks, taking, 88, 127
Water, drinking, 27, 40
Wisdom, 21, 85
Words, energy of, 38–39
Work
    60 percent rule for, 74
    career growth, 129
    drama at, 92
    vision board for, 149
Worries, reducing, 49, 106, 115, 119, 126

Yoga, 85, 86, 96–97, 134

BRING PEACE
INTO YOUR LIFE!

100
WAYS
TO
CALM

SIMPLE ACTIVITIES TO HELP YOU
FIND PEACE

PICK UP OR DOWNLOAD YOUR COPY TODAY!